PLAY WITH Paint

by Sara Lynn and Diane James

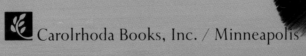

Carolrhoda Books, Inc. / Minneapolis

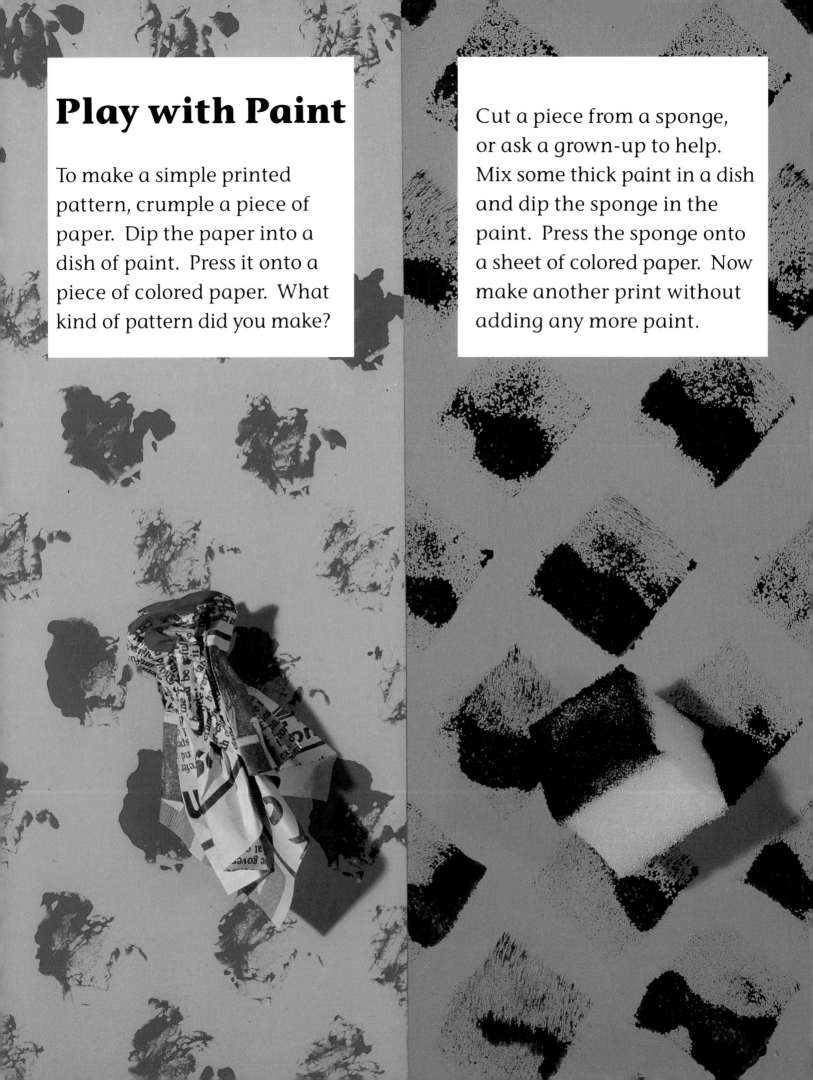

Play with Paint

To make a simple printed pattern, crumple a piece of paper. Dip the paper into a dish of paint. Press it onto a piece of colored paper. What kind of pattern did you make?

Cut a piece from a sponge, or ask a grown-up to help. Mix some thick paint in a dish and dip the sponge in the paint. Press the sponge onto a sheet of colored paper. Now make another print without adding any more paint.

To make a swirly straw painting, thin some paint with water and drip a little onto a sheet of paper. Put the end of a straw close to the paint and blow hard! Try adding a different colored paint while the first one is still wet.

Splattering is a very messy way of painting, so always put lots of newspaper down first. Dip a thick paintbrush in thin water-based paint. Flick the paintbrush over a sheet of paper—watch out for the spatters of paint. Now turn the page to try some other ideas.

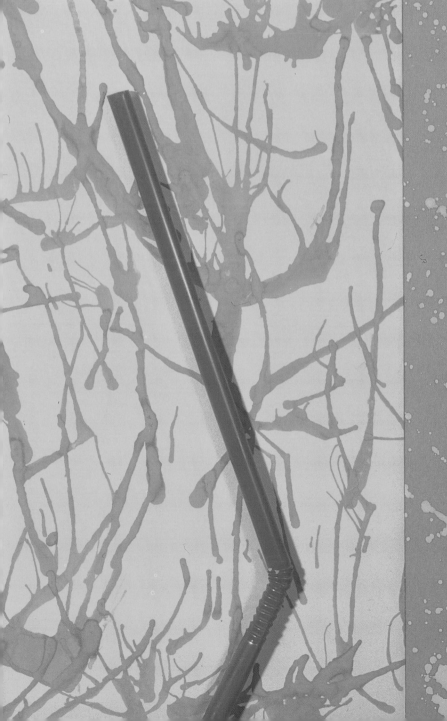

Fun Prints

You can make prints by spreading finger paint onto an object and pressing the object down on a piece of paper. Try using your finger first. We used toy building blocks, a balloon, a fork, and a plastic glue spreader. Can you think of other objects to use?

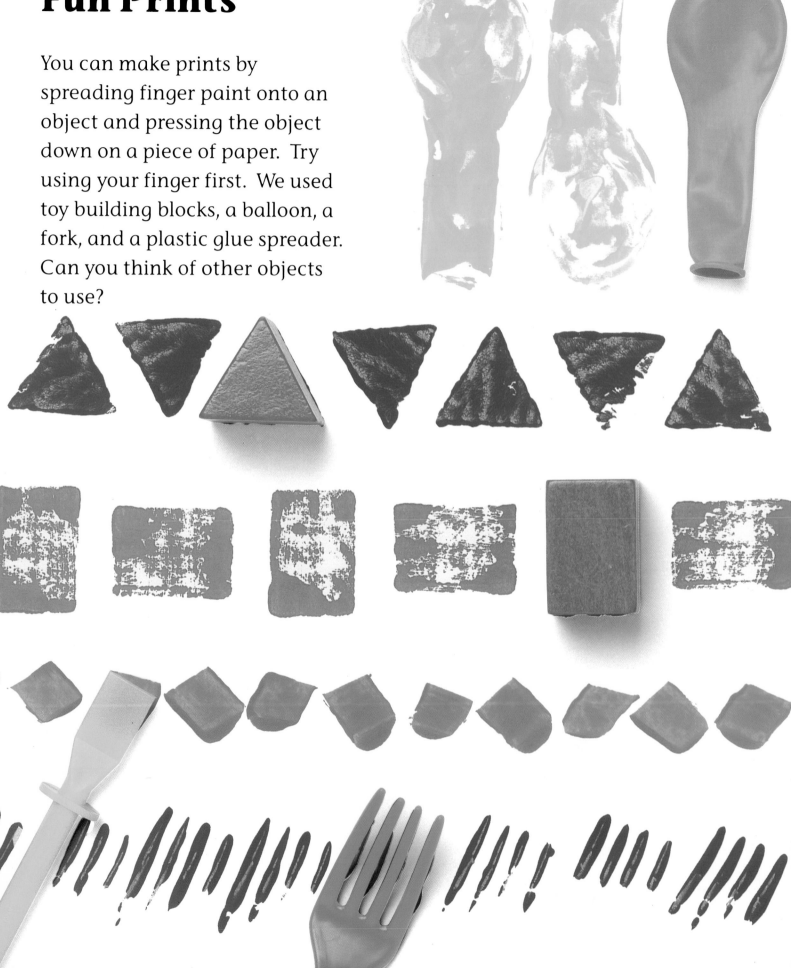

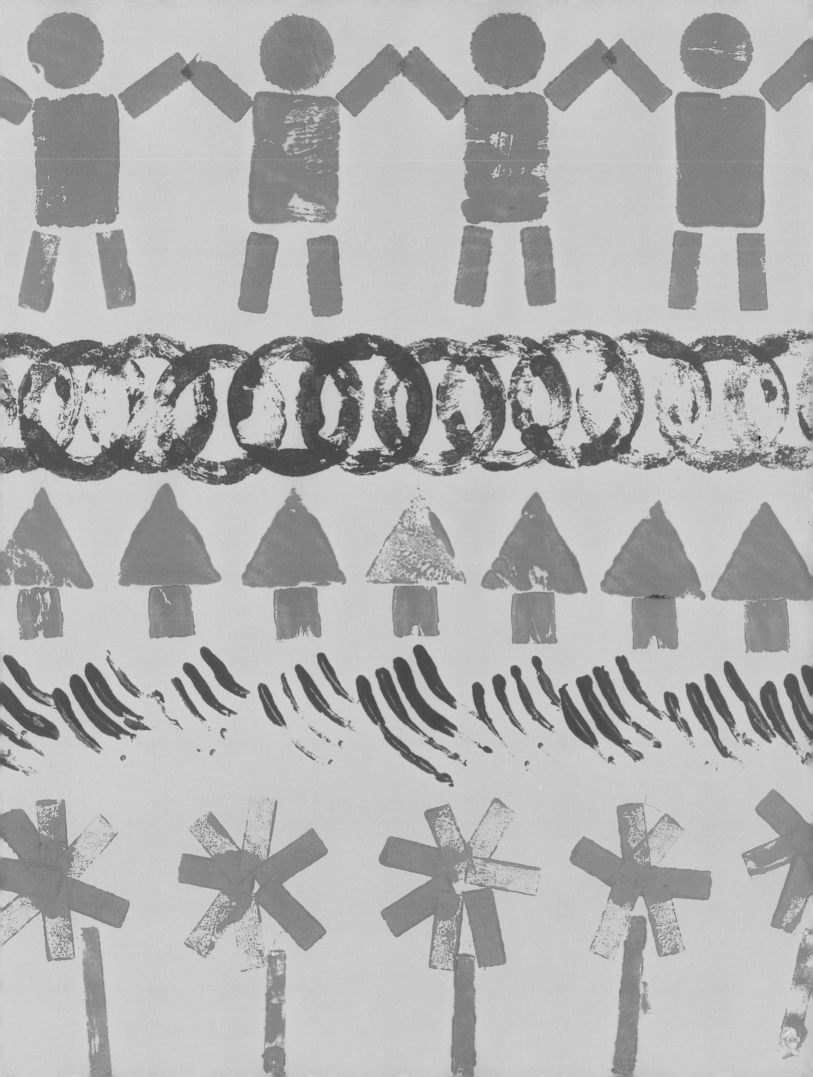

Painted Eggs

It's easy to make beautiful painted eggs like these! You'll need some hard-boiled eggs and nontoxic poster paints. You can give your painted eggs as gifts or have an egg hunt. Turn the page to find out how we made these painted eggs.

Ask a grown-up to hard-boil some eggs for you. Then let them cool. Paint the eggs all over with bright-colored poster paints. Let them dry.

Now you are ready to decorate your eggs. Think carefully about the colors you are going to use. Be sure to put lots of newspaper on the floor or table—some of these methods are messy!

We used a paintbrush with stiff bristles to paint the egg below. For this method, it is best to use a thick tempera paint. Make short brush strokes over one side of the egg—don't forget the top and bottom! When the paint is dry, turn the egg over and paint the other side the same way.

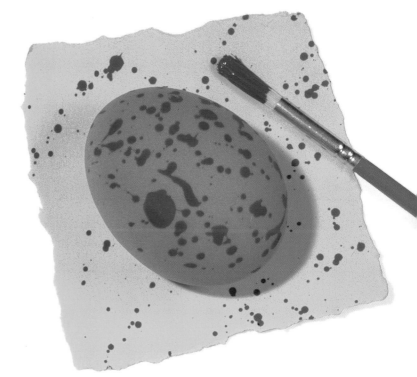

We had a lot of fun splattering paint on the egg above, but it was very messy! Put an egg on a large sheet of newspaper. Dip a paintbrush in some thin water-based paint and flick it over the egg. Splatter one side and allow it to dry before you turn the egg over to do the other side.

To decorate the egg on the right, we used a piece of crumpled paper instead of a paintbrush. Scrunch up a small piece of newspaper and dip it in some thick paint. Dab the paper onto an egg. You will need more paint after a few dabs.

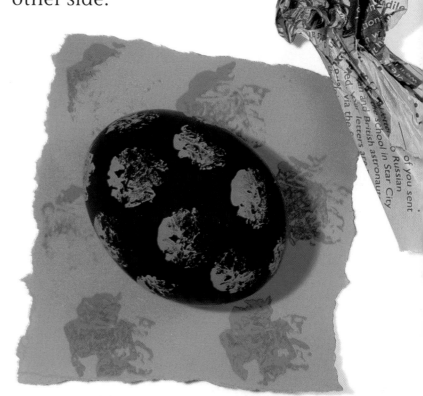

Potato Prints

Here is an easy way to make your own wrapping paper.

First, draw a shape on one half of a potato. Ask a grown-up to cut around the drawing so that the shape is raised.

Pour some paint into a dish, then dip your potato into the paint. Press the potato firmly on the paper to make a potato print! Keep printing until the paper is covered.

You can use potato prints to decorate clothes and other fabric as well as paper! To make sure your prints don't wash out, you'll need to use special fabric paints, which you can buy at a hobby shop. Keep your shapes as simple as possible. To make the happy people here, we printed green triangles on the fabric. When these were dry, we painted on the heads, arms, and legs with a paintbrush.

Macaroni Beads

These beads look almost good enough to eat! They are made from dry pasta. To make a necklace, choose a type of pasta with a hole through the middle. Paint the pasta with fairly thick paint, then thread the pieces onto thick cord or shoelaces.

You can make a necklace from bow-tie pasta by knotting thin cord around them as shown. You can also glue two kinds of pasta together to make the pretty beads below.

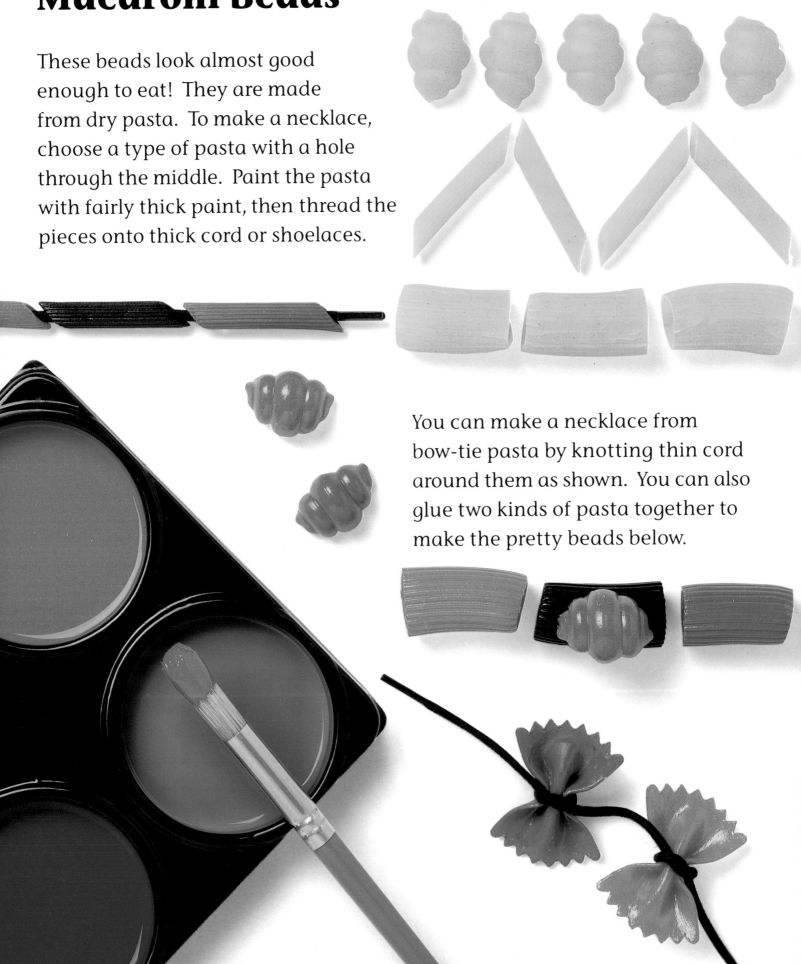

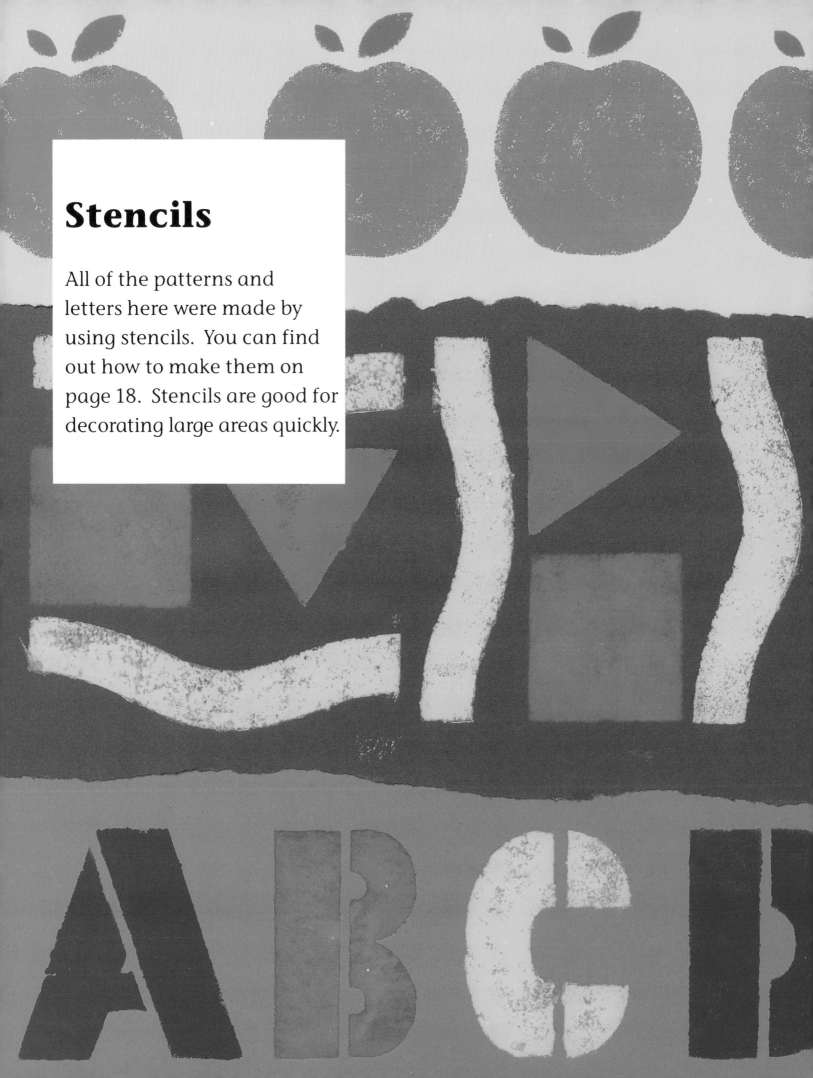

Stencils

All of the patterns and letters here were made by using stencils. You can find out how to make them on page 18. Stencils are good for decorating large areas quickly.

You could use your stencils to decorate notebook covers, or make a stencil poster. Can you think of other ways to use stencils?

You can buy sets of stencils at a store, but you can also make your own using thick cardboard. Draw a simple shape on a piece of cardboard. Ask a grown-up to cut out your shape. This is your stencil. Hold the stencil down firmly with one hand. With the other hand, dip a sponge in paint and dab it over the shape.

When you lift the stencil off, you'll see your shape! You can use stencils over and over again. Make a collection and try using different stencils to make a picture.

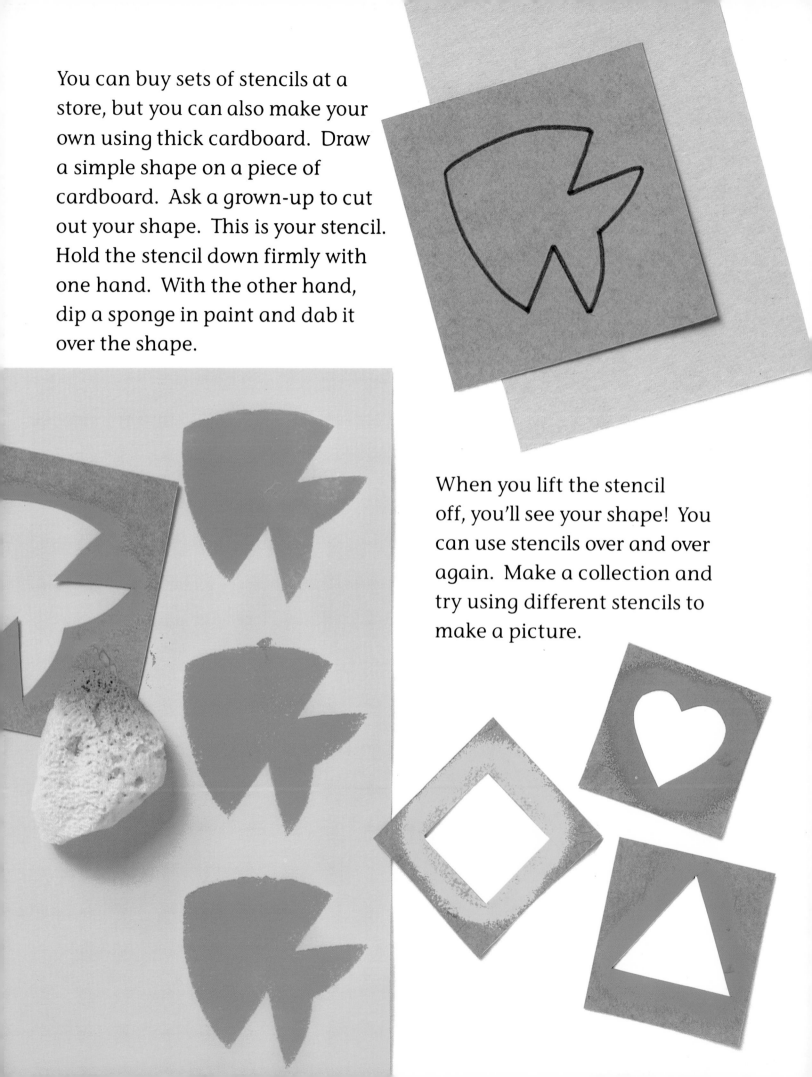

Block Prints

Here is another quick way to decorate paper. You can use printing blocks to make your own wrapping paper or a paper cover for a notebook. What else can you do with your printed paper? Turn the page to find out how we made our block prints.

You'll need some thick cardboard to make the printing blocks. Ask a grown-up to cut squares from an old corrugated cardboard box. Look for interesting shapes to glue onto your blocks. Wait until the glue is dry, then paint the blocks with thick paint.

We used thin and thick string to make the printing blocks on this page. You can glue the string down to make any shape you like. It is best for making round and swirly patterns. If you want to print with two colors, you'll have to make two printing blocks—one for each color.

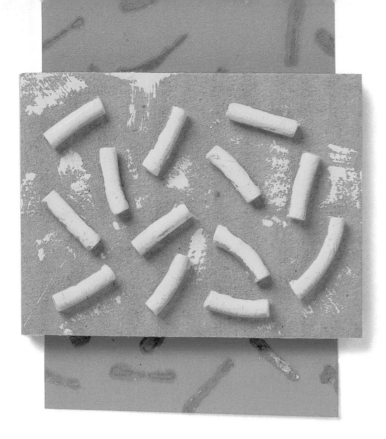

To make a pattern like the one below, ask a grown-up to cut a kitchen sponge into squares. Stick the pieces of sponge onto a printing block. Cover the pieces with thick paint and make a print.

Dry pasta makes good printing blocks and comes in all shapes and sizes. It is best to use smooth pasta rather than the kind with ridges. Try sticking dry spaghetti onto a printing block to make a striped pattern.

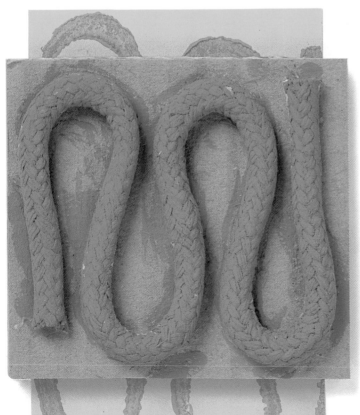

Try using two different printing blocks side by side to make an interesting pattern. You could also try printing one block on top of another, but wait for the first print to dry before adding the second. Can you think of other things that would make good printing blocks?

Photo acknowledgments: pp. 2, 3, 6, 7, 8, 9, 10, 11, Jon Barnes; pp. 4, 5, 12, 13, 14, 15, 16, 17, 18, 19, 20, 21, 22, 23, Toby.

This edition published 1993 by Carolrhoda Books, Inc.

First published in 1991 by Two-Can Publishing, 27 Cowper Street, London EC2A 4AP, UK

Library of Congress Cataloging-in-Publication Data

Lynn, Sara.
   Play with paint / Sara Lynn and Diane James.
      p.   cm.
   "First published in 1991 by Two-Can Publishing . . . London"
—T.p. verso.
   Summary: Provides instructions for using paint in a variety of ways, including prints and stencils.
   ISBN 0-87614-755-4
   1. Stencil work—Juvenile literature. 2. Paint—Juvenile literature.
3. Printing—Juvenile literature. [1. Paint. 2. Stencil work.
3. Printing] I. James, Diane. II. Title.
TT270.L96   1992
750—dc20   91-42943
                                                                  CIP
                                                                  AC

Manufactured in the United States of America

1 2 3 4 5 6 7 8 9 10 02 01 00 99 98 97 96 95 94 93